Desert Journal

Text and photographs
by Jason Edwards

PM Plus Non Fiction
Ruby

U.S. Edition © 2013 Houghton Mifflin Harcourt Publishing Company
125 High Street
Boston, MA 02110
www.hmhco.com

Text © 2003 Cengage Learning Australia Pty Limited
Illustrations © 2003 Cengage Learning Australia Pty Limited
Originally published in Australia by Cengage Learning Australia

All rights reserved. No part of this work may be reproduced or transmitted in any form or by any means, electronic or mechanical, including photocopying or recording, or by any information storage and retrieval system, without the prior written permission of the copyright owner unless such copying is expressly permitted by federal copyright law. Requests for permission to make copies of any part of the work should be submitted through our Permissions website at https://customercare.hmhco.com/contactus/Permissions.html or mailed to Houghton Mifflin Harcourt Publishing Company, Attn: Rights Compliance and Analysis, 9400 Southpark Center Loop, Orlando, Florida 32819-8647.

10   1957   20
29114

Text: Jason Edwards
Printed in China by 1010 Printing International Ltd

Acknowledgments
Photographs by Australian Picture Library/Corbis/Peter Johnson, p. 22 top/Galen Rowell, p. 14 bottom/Charles O'Rear, p. 27 top right; Getty Images/Stone, pp. 14 top, 22 Bottom. All other images by Jason Edwards/Bio-Images; Photo Researchers © George randall, p. 14 bottom left.

Desert Journal
ISBN 978 0 75 786910 5

Contents

Desert Discoveries 4

Cold Deserts 10

Hot Deserts 14

Coastal Deserts 26

My Desert Adventure 30

Glossary 32

Index 33

Desert Discoveries

Last night I had an amazing dream about deserts. Deserts have always interested me, and now I've decided to learn about them and keep a journal of my findings. My first goal? To find out exactly what a desert is!

Desert sand dunes

A desert flower

I discovered that a desert is a region with little or no water, inhabited by plants, animals, and sometimes people. Deserts receive only a small amount of rain in a year. Most cities receive more rain in only a few days!

A polar desert

Where to Find a Desert

Deserts cover nearly one third of the land surface of Earth and are found on all seven continents. If you joined all of the deserts together like a giant jigsaw puzzle, they would be large enough to cover the entire surface of the moon!

Many deserts lie around the equator, but there are also deserts in the north and south areas of the planet, and even in the huge mountain ranges of Asia and South America. There are four types of deserts:

- cold
- semi arid
- hot and dry
- coastal

Who Lives in the Desert?

When I began my research, I thought that not many plants or animals lived in deserts, but I was wrong! There are many plant and animal species that do live in deserts. Every year, scientists discover new species, and study the ways in which they survive in harsh, desert environments.

A wolf spider

Meerkats

Howling winds can whip sand into giant dunes.

Everything that lives in a desert has special ways of surviving the harsh conditions. These are called adaptations. *An adaptation helps a plant or animal survive.*

I've learned that some adaptations are easy to see — like a lizard's long toes to keep its belly off the hot sand. But others, like the anti-freeze chemical inside arctic plants, are so small we need a microscope to see them.

Coyotes that live in deserts have adapted to their harsh environment in order to survive.

The crested bicycle-dragon has long toes that help it hold its belly off the hot sand.

Not only plants and animals have found ways of surviving in the desert. Over thousands of years, people have lived in and studied the ways of the desert. People have discovered different methods of finding food, water, and shelter in these arid environments.

Solar panels collect the sun's energy and convert it to electricity. This type of energy produces no pollution.

Small towns and villages can be found in many deserts. The people who live in them are resourceful and learn to conserve water.

Cold Deserts

Not all deserts are hot and sandy. Some are frozen lands of snow and ice, drying winds, and months of darkness. These are the cold deserts. In the Arctic and Antarctica, the weather is so cold that plants and animals sometimes go without food for months. There are even places in Antarctica where no rain has fallen for two million years, and the ice is three miles thick!

The Arctic Ocean is the world's smallest ocean and is dotted with icebergs.

Antarctica is covered by a massive sheet of ice, made up of two-thirds of the world's fresh water.

People of the Ice

An Inuit hunter

For thousands of years, people have lived in the cold deserts of the north. In the Artic, the Inuit people hunt whales and seals, and fish through holes in the ice.

Antarctica is the only desert in the world where people have never lived. However, researchers now live on special bases to study the world's harshest desert. Most stay on the bases during the summer months, but some stay on through winter, in complete darkness.

An Antarctic research base

Polar bears are carnivores that eat mainly seals.

Animals of the Ice

I visited the zoo to study the polar bears. They are giants that stand twice as tall as I am! The zoo keeper told me that many polar animals *camouflage* themselves in the snow and ice. The polar bears' white coat also blends in with the ice, camouflaging them from seals and other prey. They use their great sense of smell to find their food. They wait by holes in the ice and catch seals when they surface to breathe.

Snow leopards have fur underneath their paws to keep their toes warm.

Polar animals have thick layers of fur or feathers to keep them warm. Some animals, like penguins and foxes, have a thick down that traps the heat. It is so thick that when they get wet, the skin below stays dry!

In the Arctic, the color of some birds' feathers change to match the seasons — white in winter and brown in summer. This helps them to stay camouflaged when their surroundings change.

What happens to polar animals during the dark winter months? Some go into a deep sleep called hibernation. Their body functions slow down and they stay inside dens or burrows. When spring arrives, they emerge and have a giant feast!

The ptarmigan's feathers are brown in summer and white in winter.

Hot Deserts

Midway between the equator and the north *pole* is where most *semi arid* deserts are found. *Semi arid* deserts have more rainfall and support more plant and animal life than hot and dry deserts. Temperatures in these deserts vary greatly between daytime and nighttime. Annual rainfalls range from four to twenty inches. The inhabitants of *semi arid* deserts must survive extreme weather changes.

The gila monster is a large, poisonous lizard that lives in the southwest deserts of the U.S.

The Bisti Badlands is an amazing desert area in the northwest corner of New Mexico.

Hot and dry deserts are just what they are named — the hottest, driest places on Earth. In *hot and dry* deserts, the hot air rests over the scorched earth like a blanket. The wind blows sand over animal skeletons, and mirages dance along the horizon. In Australia, *hot and dry* deserts take up almost three-quarters of the entire continent!

These deserts are kept dry by hot weather that flows around the equator and longer exposure to the sun's scorching rays. The daytime air temperature may reach 136°F, and the surface of the sand as high as 158°F!

Gemsbok live in and around sand dunes. When they die, their skeletons provide shelter for insects and trap seeds that have been blown along the sand.

Hot air shimmers on the horizon, forming a mirage.

Desert Animals

Despite the intense heat, a variety of animals live in semi arid deserts and hot and dry deserts. Life for these desert animals is spent avoiding the heat and searching for food and water.

Mammals use lots of energy. Larger mammals can store fat for emergencies, but tiny mammals need nutritious food every day. They have to be out hunting and searching all the time.

Camels store fat in their humps. They use this as fuel when food cannot be found.

Red kangaroos spend the hottest part of the day resting in the shade, to conserve water and stay cool.

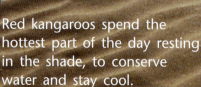

The spinifex hopping mouse never needs to drink. It has the most efficient kidneys of all mammals on earth.

Birds have an advantage over many desert animals because they can fly away from the heat. However, most birds found in the desert live there permanently. Some desert birds, such as the roadrunner, prefer to stay on the ground even though they can fly.

On the scorching sand, carnivorous insects such as spiders, scorpions, and centipedes hunt other insects. Sometimes you can hear them crunching on the bodies of their victims! Most insects feed on small fragments of plant material that the wind blows around the desert.

Scientists have estimated that all the termites living under the ground in Australia's deserts weigh more than all of the kangaroos on top of it!

Roadrunners can run as fast as 15 miles per hour.

Today, I learned that reptiles are known as *exothermic* animals. This means they rely on sunlight to raise their body temperature so they can become active. They also need the sun to warm the sand where they have laid their eggs. At night, some reptiles such as geckos go out hunting. Their bodies absorb warmth from the sand before it cools in the night air.

A barking gecko hunts at night.

Covered from head to toe in spikes, a thorny devil's body armor reminds me of a dinosaur's armor.

I also learned that snakes cannot sweat. To keep cool they weave across the baking sands, touching only a small part of their body against the hot surface. They search for shelter in the cracks of rocks, or bury themselves deep into the sand.

Even more amazing — not all frogs live in pools and streams! Some frogs make their home in the desert. They bury themselves deep in the sand where it is cool and moist. It may be several years before it rains in the desert, and then the frogs dig their way back to the surface to breed.

The death adder tricks its prey by twitching the tip of its tail. Lizards and birds think its tail is a worm and move closer. The death adder then launches from the sand and catches them.

The water-holding frog can survive underground for many years.

Desert Plants

At night, clear desert skies allow the heat to rise from the land and the temperature drops, sometimes falling below 32°F. This is when desert plants become active, as they are safe from the scorching temperatures of the day. Cactus flowers open to attract insects, and small animals emerge from their burrows to feed on them.

Desert plants may appear withered and dry, but most have special coatings to stop them from drying out. Desert plants provide food, protection, and water for the wildlife. Some have awful tasting leaves to stop animals from eating them. I made a big note in my journal to never taste desert plants again!

The nara bush has waxy coatings on its spikes and branches to help reduce water loss. Like many desert plants, they grow very slowly.

Cactus flowers open at night so they don't wilt in the harsh sun. The insects that feed on these flowers are also active at night.

Desert plants react quickly when conditions are less harsh. When it rains in hot deserts, they produce fruit and flowers. Their seeds blow around the desert for years to come. When spring comes, the plants quickly become active. They use the long daylight hours to attract insects for *pollination*.

Possibly the most impressive desert plant is the saguaro, or giant cactus, of the Southwestern United States. This huge cactus can grow up to 60 feet tall and weigh up to 10 tons.

After heavy rains, sand dunes can be covered in wild flowers.

The saguaro lives for hundreds of years. It often grows straight up for 50 years before it starts growing branches.

Desert People

The world's deserts are home to many different people. Bedouin tribes of the Middle East march their camels across the hot sands from one oasis to the next. Africa's bush tribes hunt animals and dig up roots and tubers for water. The Navajo and Pueblo tribes have lived in the southwestern deserts of the U.S. for over 1,000 years.

African bushmen hunt for food.

Australia's Aboriginals have wandered the vast outback for over 40,000 years, learning the ways of the desert.

Many of the world's deserts are scattered with ghost towns, but today more people live in deserts than ever before. In some cases, they even have air conditioning and farms with irrigation. Satellites tell farmers where fresh grass is growing so they can graze their cattle.

People still live in traditional mud houses in Acoma Pueblo, New Mexico, which is one of the oldest continuously inhabited settlements in North America.

In the Mandawa Desert of India, houses are built of straw, and then covered in clay to keep the interior cool.

Case Study: Death Valley

Death Valley National Park does not have a name that inspires most people to visit it. Yet this land of contrasts and extremes does have life and a beauty all its own.

Located in east California, Death Valley is the hottest and driest place in the U.S. It has an average rainfall of about two inches for the entire year. Temperatures of $125°F$ are common during the summer. Visitors usually avoid Death Valley in the summer, choosing to visit in the winter or spring instead.

The national park includes the valley and surrounding mountains. Death Valley is 130 miles long and very deep. It contains the lowest point in the Western Hemisphere. This spot near Badwater is 282 feet below sea level.

The lowest point in the Western Hemisphere is in Death Valley and is 282 feet below sea level.

The mountains that surround Death Valley rarely allow rain to get to the valley.

Despite its name, many things live in the park. More than 1,000 kinds of plants live there. The plants on the valley floor have adapted to living in the desert. Some have roots that go down 40-50 feet, while the roots of others are shallow but extend out widely.

The animals that live in the valley are mainly active at night. They include bobcats, coyotes, foxes, reptiles, and squirrels.

25

Coastal Deserts

Rare and fragile coastal deserts are found on the rugged coastlines of Africa and South America. Sailors have feared these coastlines for centuries and many ships have been wrecked there on stormy nights.

Icy water flowing north from Antarctica chills the sea, and giant fogbanks form along the coast. The fog moves inland carrying moisture to plants and animals in the desert. The fog only lasts several hours, but this is enough to support life in these coastal deserts.

A giant fogbank moves inland across a coastal desert.

A shipwreck on the African coast

Mountains near the ocean often prevent moisture from moving inland, and deserts form in their shadow. This is known as the rain-shadow effect.

On the coast of South America, this rain-shadow effect is reversed. Moisture is trapped inland by the Andes mountains and falls as rain on the Amazon rainforests. South America's Atacama Desert has therefore formed along the coast.

The Atacama Desert, in South America

Africa's Namib Desert is also a coastal desert, and has a mountain range made of sand. These sand dunes are the tallest in the world, towering over 900 feet. Sailors call this coastline the Skeleton Coast because of the huge number of ships and people that have been lost there.

If sailors survived a shipwreck, a more grisly fate awaited them in the baking desert. Many did not survive.

Sand dunes in the Namib Desert

Coastal Desert Animals

This is the only species of white beetle in the world. It is found in Africa's coastal deserts. It marches over the gravel plains on its long legs, and survives by drinking the moisture from fog which collects on its body.

Black-backed jackals hunt the birds living on an abandoned oil rig. They wait for chicks to fall out of the nests.

Many coastal desert animals visit seal colonies by the desert shore to find food. The seals frolic in the seas, feeding on fish and squid. Birds search for scraps of fish, and black-backed jackals search for seal pups or chicks to feed on.

Further inland, beetles collect water by standing on their heads in the morning fog. Moisture in the fog forms drops of water that run down their bodies and into their mouths. Lizards and snakes also use the fog. Lizards lick water drops off rocks and snakes lick their scales where moisture from the fog has collected.

Magellan penguins in Patagonia are the only penguins to nest in a desert. They dig a burrow in the hard earth for their chicks, and walk to the ocean to find food.

Elephants live in Africa's Namib Desert. They not only use their ears for hearing over large distances, but also for fanning themselves to stay cool.

One of the most amazing things I have discovered is that there are elephants living on the Skeleton Coast in Africa. They survive by finding water buried in dry riverbeds and inside plants. Once lions inhabited the Skeleton Coast. They hunted for food on the beaches and in the sand dunes. Sadly they were all killed by poachers and villagers.

My Desert Adventure

By writing this journal, I have learned so much about deserts and how fragile they are. Deserts can be frightening and dangerous places, but also full of adventure.

There are certain times of the year when it's best to visit a desert. For a hot desert, it is best to visit in winter when temperatures are cooler. For cooler deserts, spring and autumn are the best times. Early morning and late afternoon are ideal for exploring. More animals are active at these times, and the temperature will be cooler than during the middle of the day. Night time is also a great time to go exploring, as many animals are out feeding.

Like any outdoor activity, safety should come first. My desert kit includes good walking shoes, a hat, sun lotion, and comfortable cotton pants and a shirt. I always carry a water bottle, and never go walking anywhere without telling someone where I am going, and when I'll return.

Happy deserting!

Glossary

adaptations	*the way a plant or animal changes to become better suited to its environment*
Antarctica	*the frozen continent at the South Pole*
Arctic	*the area around the North Pole*
arid	*very dry*
camouflage	*to hide by blending with the environment*
coastal	*deserts located near the coast*
down	*an extra insulating layer under an animal's fur or feathers, that traps heat*
equator	*an imaginary line around the middle of the Earth*
exothermic	*relying on an external source of heat to keep warm*
hibernation	*spending the winter in a deep sleep, and not waking up until the weather gets warmer*
poles	*the two locations at the North and South ends of Earth*
pollination	*a process where pollen is deposited in a flower or plant to allow fertilization*
rain-shadow	*an effect that creates a dry area of land. Rain cannot fall due to mountains blocking its path*
semi arid	*deserts that are hot in sumer and cold in winter*
tubers	*roots or parts of a stem found underground*